L for the lavender over the bed
M for the man that I love
N for the nasty bits stuck in the sink
O for the wings of a dove

BIRD DROPPING

SIMON DREW'S
BEST
OF BIRDS

THE BANTAM OF THE OPERA

DRAWINGS AND VERSES
BY SIMON DREW

ANTIQUE COLLECTORS' CLUB

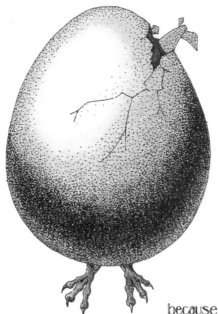

because a bird has no placenta
eggs is how this world they enter

to Caroline,
and to my parents
without whom none of me
would have been possible.

© 1996 Simon Drew   ISBN 1 85149 245 3
World copyright reserved

British Library Cataloguing-in-Publication Data
A catalogue record for this book is available from the British Library

The illustrations in this book have been taken from three earlier works by Simon Drew:
The Book of Bestial Nonsense (1986), *Nonsense in Flight* (1987), and *The Puffin's Advice*
(1989), all of which are now out of print.

The right of Simon Drew to be identified as author of this work has been asserted by
him in accordance with the Copyright, Design and Patents Act 1988

Published and printed in England by the Antique Collectors' Club Ltd., Woodbridge,
Suffolk IP12 1DS on Consort Royal Satin paper from Donside Mills, Aberdeen

INTRODUCTION

Some people are unaware of some of the extraordinary properties possessed by birds. This group of the animal kingdom is such a strange collection of beasts that they could never have been invented by any human being. Any inventor of merit could never have forgotten arms, for instance; can you imagine designing an animal which is so superb at flying and then forgetting to give it arms and hands for manipulating whatever it has just flown to? Look at the ridiculous way that an egyptian vulture breaks an egg (to eat its contents) by randomly lobbing a stone into the air from its beak.

Could anyone ever have dreamt up the comical absurdities of the puffin, secretary bird, blue stork or penguin?

Obviously evolution has been in progress, resulting in the irregular beings that we know. It is not generally known that the horse evolved from the peacock: this bird used to have the curious habit of landing upside down on its tail feathers. A few birds of the species stayed this way up and passed the characteristic on to their offspring. Illustrated here is the intermediary species which is capable of remaining in either position:

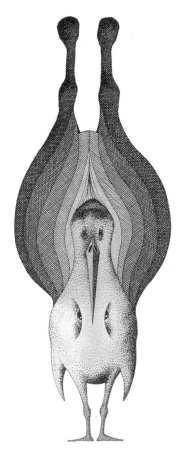

the wily gannet sits on granite
thus avoiding germs
and so this bird must feed on fish
for granite has no worms.

FRANCE'S DRAKE

WATER OFF A DUCK'S BACK

The birds below have almost reached extinction:
not killed by fire or storm or tremor,
but wrangling politicians of distinction
impaled them on the horns of a dilemma.

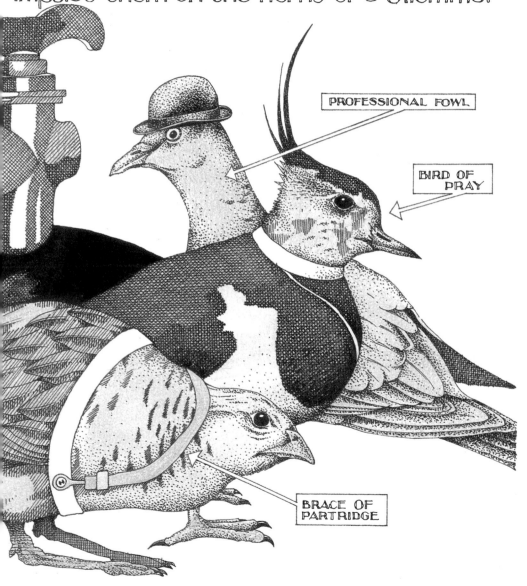

PROFESSIONAL FOWL

BIRD OF PRAY

BRACE OF PARTRIDGE

PUFFIN

waders

12

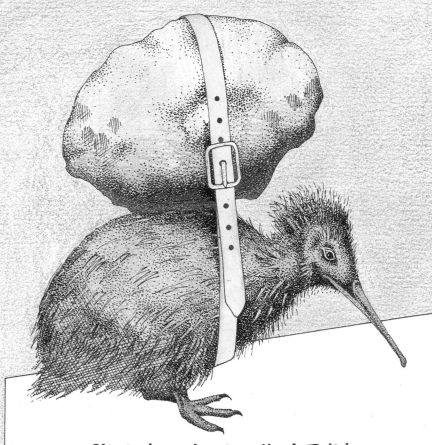

a flightless bird called Faith
began to carry boulders:
for years she took these weights
strapped between her shoulders;
and as you might expect
the sweat poured like a fountain,
but only time will tell
if Faith can move a mountain.

PENGUIN DE MILO

drew

A PARROT ON A PERCH

18

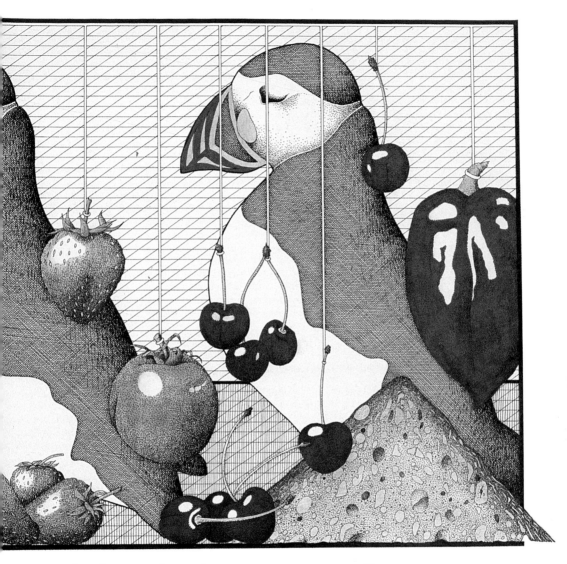

A cherry's a berry to eat on its own.
In the soft centre you'll find there's a stone,
once it's removed you must eat the flesh whole
for these are the fruits of which life is a bowl.

BREAKFAST, PART ONE

On Tuesday last, without a sound
I'd woken, dressed and gone downstairs
expecting breakfast, but I found
a sight that took me unawares.

The sugar bowl showed signs of feet,
the butter's state you'd call distressed,
the marmalade was far from neat,
and someone had consumed the rest.

BREAKFAST, PART TWO

Today I rose and dressed in haste,
brought in the milk and fetched the post.
I tucked my shirt tails in my waist
and dreamed of scrambled egg on toast.

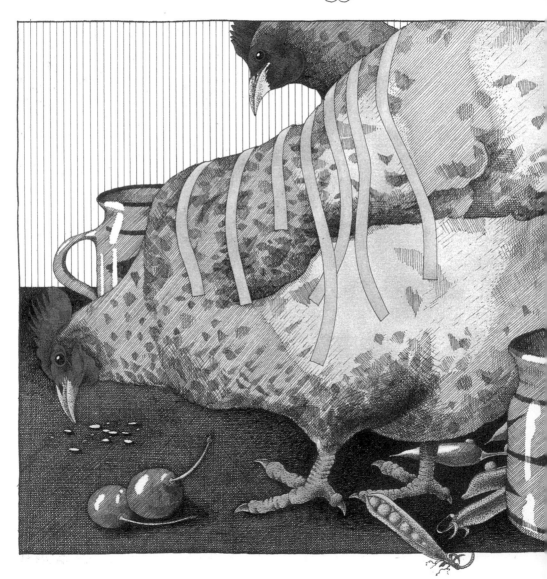

I found there'd been another raid:
(I caught a glimpse of running legs).
The table had been neatly laid
and so had half a dozen eggs.

THE EVENING DEAR ADA PASSED AWAY

It was after the pastor had said the last rites,
the rooster came in here and turned off the lights;
(and so this is one of those memorable sights
we often recall on the long winter nights).

Le déjeuner sur l'herbe avec deux canards

swan up, duck down, fish out, larks about

IN PRAISE OF FISHY DINNERS

From the depth of souls and oceans
can it be denied:
any bird that lives on herring
must have brains inside.

HOW TO PUT A SHIP IN A BOTTLE...

1

First of all you fetch some paper
wood and bits of string:
then construct the perfect schooner,
strength must be the thing.

2

Now a bottle: this is crucial.
Don't pick one too thin.
If you're making something special
choose one made for gin.

3

But this bottle must be empty
(letting in the boat).
Place the contents in a tumbler
then transfer to throat.

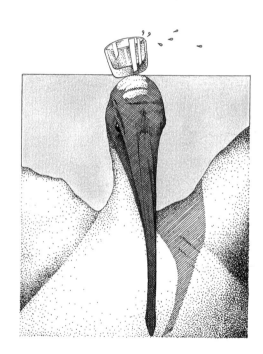

4

Now you'll sing a rousing chorus
as you dance a jig;
(though the ship's not in the bottle
you won't give a fig).

THE PUFFIN'S ADVICE

Advice for the single or the married — or those thinking of changing from one to the other.

A robin was once in love with a wren:
they wanted to marry but didn't know when.

34

So they went to a puffin to ask his advice.
He said to them: "Listen, I won't say this twice:

wait till you see a thrush in a stocking,

and naked mute swans
(but don't find it shocking),

and when you find avocets drinking brown ale,

and light fingered parrots that end up in jail,

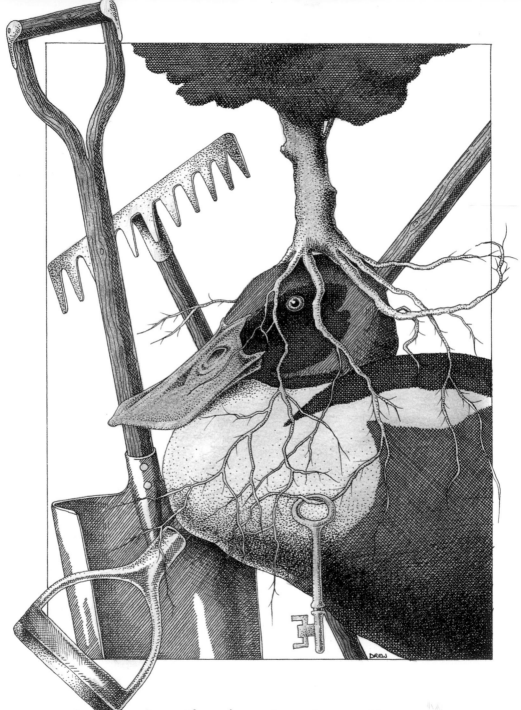

and   when there's a shoveler rooting up trees
while seeking its purse that it lost with its keys,

and when spotted parakeets sit on your phone
and ask if you're able to give them a loan,

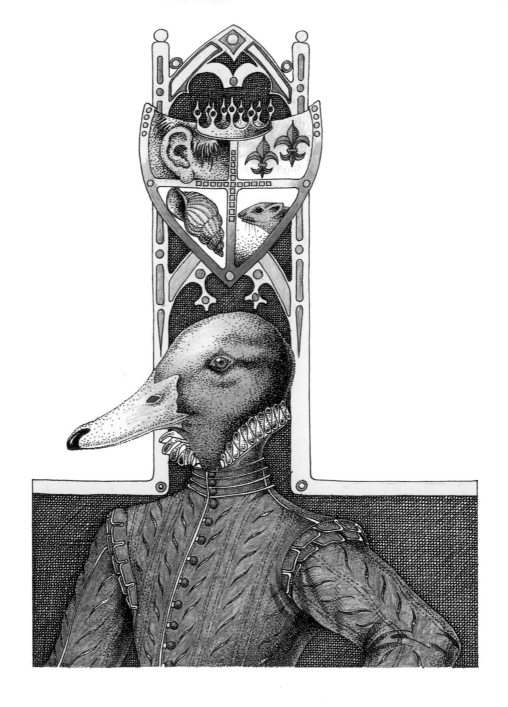

and when there's a mallard that claims it's an earl,

and nuthatches dive in the sea for a pearl,

and when you see sparrows in deep conversation,

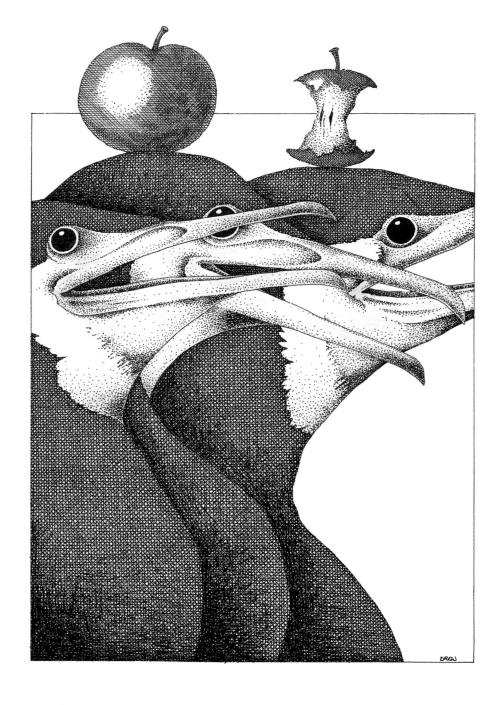

and cormorants laughing with no explanation,

and when there   are emus in blazers and boaters
whose kneecaps are fitted with powerful motors,

and when all the magpies
                    are too fat to carry
that is the time I advise you to marry."

EIDER WAY UP

EIDER WAY UP

THE DIFFERENCE BETWEEN A SHOE AND A DUCK

You will notice a shoe has a leather cross-section
and ducks leave unbearable dung.
(To distinguish the two by internal inspection
is hard, for they both have a tongue).